Turtles, Frogs, Snakes and Lizards
Children's Science & Nature

BABY PROFESSOR

EDUCATION KIDS

Check out amazing facts about reptiles and amphibians. Let's talk about turtles, frogs, snakes, and lizards. Read on and get into their amazing world!

Reptiles are amazing animals covered with scales. They are characterized by their skins, which are made up of bony, overlapping plates, like armor. Most reptiles are cold blooded and lay eggs.

TURTLES. These amazing reptiles have existed for at least 215 million years. Turtles are protected by their hard shell. It is their shield. The carapace refers to the upper shell. The lower shell is known as the plastron.

Most turtles hide their heads inside their shell when they are attacked by predators.

The largest turtle is the
leatherback sea turtle.
It weighs over 900
kg. Many turtles lay
their eggs in the sand.
They just leave their
eggs, and when the
babies are born they
know to go downhill
to the water and start
to swim. Turtles are
endangered today.

SNAKES. Snakes are meat eaters. They just swallow their food since they can't chew it the way we can. They are capable of eating very large animals. Amazingly, snakes have flexible jaws which allow them to swallow food that seems bigger than they are themselves.

Snakes come in approximately 3000 different species. These reptiles don't have eyelids. Their ears are internal. They have scales as their body coverings. Snakes use their tongues for smelling.

Some snakes are deadly and are venomous. Examples of them are cobras and black mambas. They kill their prey with their venom. Anacondas are large snakes which thrive in South America. The longest snakes in the world are the pythons.

LIZARDS. It is believed that there are over 3,000 lizard species in the world. They can be found anywhere except in the polar regions. Most lizards live in trees. Some live on the ground and only a few live in the water.

Lizards have eyelids and long tails. Most of them have four legs. A group of lizards that has no legs is called amphisbaenas.

Among the species of lizards, only a few are poisonous. These include the Gila monster and the beaded lizard. They are found in the North American deserts.

One of the largest
lizards is the Komodo
Dragon. It has sharp
teeth for biting, and it
also deposits poison in
its prey when it bites.

Lizards come in different colors. Some are brightly-colored. Some use camouflage to blend with their surroundings. Examples of these are the chameleons. They can change their skin color to match their surroundings.

What are amphibians? They are ancient vertebrates that live both on land and in the water, and may have been the first vertebrates that ever existed on Earth. Amphibians use their five senses just like human beings. However, they can detect the Earth's magnetic field and see ultraviolet light.

Amphibians are cold-blooded. The temperature of their bodies changes when the temperature of their surroundings changes. They are also vertebrates, like birds, mammals, reptiles and fish. They have backbones.

Examples of amphibians are salamanders, toads, frogs, newts and caecilians.

Say hello to the hopping frogs! Frogs are amphibians. Frogs lay their eggs in round bunches. Amazingly, each bunch contains over 500 eggs! These are clear jelly eggs. After a day or two, each egg starts to look like a tadpole.

Frogs molt often to keep their skin thin and fresh. They do this by eating their skin around their mouths. Frogs, just like toads, make a croaking sound to attract their mates.

The Cuban tree frog is
the smallest amphibian
we know of. It grows
up to 12mm in length,
or just half an inch.
The largest of all the
amphibians are the
Japanese and Chinese
giant salamanders.

Did you enjoy
reading about reptiles
and amphibians?
Share this to
your friends.

Visit
BABY PROFESSOR
EDUCATION KIDS
www.BabyProfessorBooks.com
to download Free Baby Professor eBooks
and view our catalog of new and exciting
Children's Books